The Secret Diary of A Sc

SUE TOWNSEND

music and lyrics by
KEN HOWARD
and
ALAN BLAIKLEY

musical arrangements by
MARK WARMAN

illustrations by
CAROLINE HOLDEN

Methuen

Contents

Also by Sue Townsend:

The Secret Diary of Adrian Mole Aged 13¾
The Growing Pains of Adrian Mole
Bazaar and Rummage, Groping for Words and Womberang
The Great Celestial Cow
The Secret Diary of Adrian Mole Aged 13¾: The Play

The songs in this volume are taken from the stage version of *The Secret Diary of Adrian Mole Aged 13¾: The Play* of which the text is published by Methuen. They are also available on an EMI record and cassette, EJ24 02601: Sue Townsend's *The Secret Record of Adrian Mole*, music and lyrics produced by Ken Howard and Alan Blaikley

First published in 1985
by Methuen London Ltd
11 New Fetter Lane, London EC4P 4EE

Made and printed in Great Britain
by Hazell Watson & Viney Ltd
Member of the BPCC Group
Aylesbury, Bucks

ISBN 0 413 59690 7 (hardback)
0 413 59700 8 (paperback)

Dog food
Badedas
Tea
Cod in Parsley Sauce
(in bag)
Coke (for sniffing ha ha)
Cigarettes
Bacon
Gin

The House Where I Live

I felt rotten today. It's my mother's fault for singing 'My Way' at two o'clock in the morning at the top of the stairs. There is a chance my parents could be alcoholics. Next year I could be in a children's home.

The spot on my chin is getting bigger. It's my mother's fault for not knowing about vitamins.

Could I, the same Adrian Mole, who is in almost weekly correspondence with the luminous John Tydeman of the BBC, have written the above extracts? The blood rushes to my acne-scarred cheeks when I reread my old diary. Still, *non, je ne regrette rien*, as they say in the frog language.

At the callow age of thirteen and three-quarters I fell, mesmerised, under the mesmerising spell of a singing French dwarf called Charles Aznavour. My mother, Pauline, had bought his LP at the Co-op in a moment of *ennui* while waiting at the check-out. The mournful sound of French singing filled our semi for a fortnight until my mother, fickle as always, forgot about Charles and turned to Tina Turner.

However, I was morbidly attached by now to the throbbing self-pity of the French style of singing. It perfectly suited my nihilistic attitude to life which was brought on by my parents' crumbling marriage, for they were too busy arguing about trivialities, like who left a slice of bacon on the floor between the fridge and the cooker, to bother about me and my thirteen-and-three-quarter-year-old angst.

ADRIAN

She doesn't cook me my meals,
Doesn't know how it feels
To be hungry and young:
And he doesn't budge from his chair,
Doesn't care if I'm here – or there!

Yes, this is my family seat,
Eighteen Every Street –
It's the house where I live.

They ought to care if I smoke,
Ask if I'm sniffing coke,
Disapprove of my friends:
I could be in some gangster's pay
Or be wasting away, day by day!

While they sit there sunk in their gloom
I could meet with my doom
In the house where I live.

No cheerful fire in our hearth,
Badedas in our bath,
Aerosol in the loo:
Who sees if we've run out of tea?
Or the dog's done a pee? – It's me!

Yes, here in its bleak monochrome
Is my own broken home,
It's the house where I live.
Yes, this is my own broken home,
It's the house where I live.

Moderato

ADRIAN:

She _____ doesn't cook me my
They _____ ought to care if I
No _____ cheerful fire in our

meals, _____ Doesn't know how it feels _____ To be hung-ry and
smoke, _____ Ask if I'm snif-fing coke, _____ Dis - ap - prove of my
hearth, _____ Ba - de - das in our bath, _____ Aer - o - sol in the

5

Nothing In Common

MRS LUCAS How was I mad enough to think
There could ever be a link
Between Bimbo and me?
We were two ships that should have passed,
Steaming onwards very fast
Through the night. God – how right
To have missed out on Mr Wrong long
before this
Sour history of dissonance was ever
conceived!

Who but a loser could have won
Such a barrel-load of fun,
Such a prize, such a stud!
This dud – did he sparkle at the start?
Did I really think him smart,
Think him wise, think him kind?
How blind, how obtuse I was – he's useless
and crass:
We're out of sync, out of tune – and I'm
out of my mind!

MR LUCAS	MRS LUCAS
Don't you have a drain to fix?	We're out of sync,
Or some concrete to mix?	We're out of tune.
You're in my way,	Out of tune.
Go away!	Out of tune.
Go away!	

MRS LUCAS I go for yoga and Gestalt,
Bran, high-fibre, yeast and malt,
Monteverdi and Bach . . .

MR LUCAS (reading from a glossy magazine)
Andrew Lloyd-Webber!

MRS LUCAS I'm into Greenham and Greenpeace,
Shelter, NACRO and Release,
Purer air, pedal power!

MR LUCAS (reading) Saab Turbo 900!

MRS LUCAS You bore me and appal me like no-one else
can:
But then I'm a woman, and you're – just a
man!

MR LUCAS Right!

MRS LUCAS What?

MR LUCAS Go!

MRS LUCAS Right!

MR LUCAS Go!

MRS LUCAS Right!

MR AND MRS LUCAS Right!

Mr Lucas was in the kitchen drinking coffee with my mother. The room was full of smoke. They were laughing, but when I went in they stopped. Mrs Lucas was next-door cleaning the drains. She looked as if she was in a bad mood. I think Mr and Mrs Lucas have got an unhappy marriage. Poor Mr Lucas!

Rat-fink Lucas has wrought havoc on our family since I innocently penned the above words. He stole my mother and took her to Sheffield and, although my mother came home again, Lucas is still in contact with our family.

Dear Moles: Adrian, George, but especially Pauline.
Yes, it's your old friend Bimbo Lucas writing to you again. Thought I'd forgotten all about you, eh? No way. You have ruined my life. I was once content to be a suburbanite, never happier than when I was watching the wife wash the car on Sunday mornings. Then neighbourly overtures were made. I remember George coming round to borrow a socket set (which, incidentally, I never got back); next it was Adrian to borrow a cup of monosodium glutamate; then finally and fatally Pauline, the temptress, in her cut-off blue jeans and jokey tee-shirt. The die was cast. Pauline and I were creatures of fate; autumn leaves sucked into the vortex. Pebbles disturbed by the tide. My poor wife, realising that she couldn't keep me, turned in her despair to her own sex for comfort and companionship. At least that's my theory.
So here I sit, writing to you at a second-hand executive work station in my cold flat in Sheffield. Alone, unloved, and wifeless, with only the memories of mine and Pauline's mad affair to keep me from tying the noose around my neck.
Yours in bitter enmity,
Bimbo Lucas

P.S. Had a postcard from Mrs Lucas. She didn't write much. I quote: 'Will you donate your dreadful gold medallions and chunky bracelets to the cause of Peace? We are holding an auction. You owe me £15,000, my half of the sale of *our* house!'

It was postmarked 'Molesworth'.

Nothing In Common

MRS. LUCAS: I'm go for yo - ga and Ge -

- stalt, bran, high fi-bre, yeast and malt, Mon - te - ver - di and Bach. _____

MR. LUCAS: An-drew Lloyd Web-ber!

MRS. LUCAS:
I'm in - to Greenham and Green peace, Shel - ter, Nac - ro and Re - lease, pur - er air, ped - al -

I Know What Women Like

MR LUCAS

She talks about her married life –
Her husband's perfect,
She's the faithful wife:
She says 'Please understand'
But doesn't move my hand –
I know what women like.

She phones to say she feels half-dead –
She'll take a Valium
And go to bed:
But if I say 'Okay'
She says 'Come anyway' –
I know what women like.

They're predictably contrary
And reliably perverse;
When they say 'I really mean it'
They mean really the reverse;
They say they want to hear the truth,
No flattery or lies;
But the 'truth' must be they're beautiful,
Desirable and wise.

She talks about her married life –
Her husband's perfect,
She's the faithful wife . . .
I know what women like.

Tuesday March 24th

Late last night I saw my mother and Mr Lucas going out in Mr Lucas's car. They went somewhere special because my mother was wearing a boiler suit with sequins. She did look a bit wanton. Mr Lucas was wearing his best suit, and he had a lot of gold jewellery on. For an old person he certainly knows how to dress. If my father took more care of his appearance, none of this would have happened. It stands to reason that any woman would prefer a man to wear a suit and a lot of gold jewellery, to one like my father who hardly ever shaves and wears old clothes and no jewellery.

Midnight *Mother still not home.*

2 a.m. *No sign of my mother.*

I mourn for my lost innocence as exemplified above.

Lucas's estimation of what women like is based on surreptitious visits to the Palais de Dance on 'Over Twenty-Fives' Night. There may be a few women who will give away their virginity after one glimpse of a gold Dunhill lighter, but they are a dying breed. I am now an authority on women. I have made a list of what they like:

Kittens
Flowers
Terry's 'All Gold' Chocolates
Sad, clever men who are unshaven and wear old clothes
Other women
Roger and Gallet soap
Books by Fay Weldon
Expensive boots
Having careers

I Know What Women Like

like. They're pre - dic - tab - ly con - trar - y And re - li - a - bly per - verse, When they

Faster

say 'I real - ly mean it' They mean real - ly the re - verse: They say they want to hear the truth, No

flat - ter - y or lies; But the 'truth' must be they're beau - ti - ful, De - sir - a - ble and wise.

rall.

Freely

She talks a-bout her mar-ried l life — Her hus-band's per-fect, She's the

faith - ful wife. . . I know what wo - men like. I ___ know what

wo - men like.

Sorry Gotta Do It

BARRY KENT

Sorry, gotta do it, gotta do it,
Sorry, gotta do it,
Sorry, gotta do it, gotta do it, gotta do it:
Nothing personal – know what I mean?

What you need is my protection:
In return I take collection
Of a paltry pound or three – it
Makes good sense! Invest in me! Like

You're the client, I'm the banker:
I need finance, you're a wanker!
Things are as they ought to be, now
I've got you and you've got me – see?

Sorry, gotta do it, gotta do it,
Sorry, gotta do it,
Sorry, gotta do it, gotta do it, gotta do it:
Nothing personal – know what I mean?

Breathe a word and you'll regret it!
Think of squealing? Don't forget, it's
Me you'll have to answer to – and
In the end, I *will* get you! I'll

Have your little guts for garters,
Mash your face in – just for starters!
'Cause you know my golden rule is
No holds barred – go for the goolies!

Sorry, gotta do it, gotta do it,
Sorry, gotta do it,
Sorry, gotta do it, gotta do it, gotta do it:
Nothing personal – know what I mean?

Tuesday March 3rd
SHROVE TUESDAY

I gave Barry Kent his protection money today. I don't see how there can be a God. If there was surely he wouldn't let people like Barry Kent walk about menacing intellectuals? Why are bigger youths unpleasant to smaller youths? Perhaps their brains are easily worn out with all the extra work they have to do making bigger bones and stuff, or it could be that the big youths have got brain damage because of all the sport they play, or perhaps big youths just like *menacing and fighting. When I go to university I may study the problem.*

I will have my thesis published and I will send a copy to Barry Kent. Perhaps by then he will have learnt to read.

If only I had known in 1981 what I know now.

That Barry Kent suffers from 'arachnophobia', the morbid fear of spiders. A spider in a matchbox would have been the perfect bodyguard. As soon as I saw B.K. stamping into view I could have opened the matchbox and let my hairy eight-legged protector on to the back of my hand. B.K.'s brutal shaved head would have paled. His tight denimed body would have tensed, his knobbly fists would have slackened and he would have turned and run away in his bully-boy brown Doc Martens. However, that is all in the past.

B.K. and I are now quite good friends. Barry was taught to write poetry at a Detention Centre, by a louche Poet in Residence. Some of his efforts are almost good.

Crime and Punishment by Baz Kent

OK, so I nicked it.
So what?
It was there.
Like what the mountaineer said.
I took the object from one place to another place.
My place.
OK, so they locked me up.
So what?
They took my body from one place to another place.
Their place.
Even Stevens, eh?

Sorry Gotta Do It

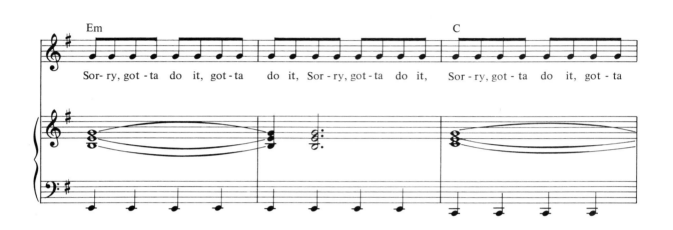

Sor-ry, got-ta do it, got-ta do it, Sor-ry, got-ta do it, Sor - ry, got-ta do it, got-ta

do it, got-ta do it: Noth-ing per-son-al know what I mean?

The Bad Old Days

BERT

When I was just your age, son,
When I was just a lad,
Things were far different then
I can tell you, my friend –
They were ten times as bad!
Had me no gilded youth, boy,
Lit by no sunshine rays –
We were fourteen in a hovel,
Takin' lessons how to grovel,
In the bad old days.

Lenin's my hero still, boy,
He was a man of steel:
If he came back today
His hair would turn grey
At the whole lousy deal!
Paid up and joined the Party,
Carried the big red flag:
We were comrades in an army,
Though they told us we were barmy,
In the bad old days.

We toiled our youth away, boy,
No money, no thanks, no praise:
They say, 'Where there's muck
  there's brass –'
I say, 'Not on your bloomin' arse!'
They were bad old days.

Monday September 28th
NEW MOON

Bert has got something wrong with his legs. The doctor says he needs daily nursing. I went in today, but he is too heavy for me to lug about. The district nurse thinks that Bert will be better off in the Alderman Cooper Sunshine Home. But I don't think he will. I pass by it on my way to school. It looks like a museum. The old people look like the exhibits.

> *Bert, you are dead old.*
> *Fond of Sabre, beetroot and Woodbines.*
> *We have nothing in common,*
> *I am fourteen and a half,*
> *You are eighty-nine.*
> *You smell, I don't.*
> *Why we are friends*
> *Is a mystery to me.*

Bert is still alive; he is now ninety-two or ninety-three – nobody knows for sure. Bert's survival has got nothing to do with medical science. He won't have anything to do with doctors or nurses. On the grounds that 'I don't like having me privates mauled about.' No. Bert refuses to die until he sees the English masses rise up and have a revolution, and take over the management of the *Daily Express* and the Stock Exchange. He is the only nonagenarian to have joined the picket-line during the miners' strike. His lusty shouts of 'Scab! Scab!' turned quite a few working miners back to the soup kitchens. Also he was a formidable collector of money in the town centre. His wheelchair was festooned with collecting tins. I used to dread the journey back to the striking miners' headquarters: the weight of Bert and the full money tins almost killed me. Pushing a wheelchair containing a fourteen-stone old man and six full money tins is no easy matter. Still, I can't help but admire Bert for sticking to his creed when all around are rejecting theirs and joining the SDP.

Bert is always on at me to join the Party but so far I have resisted. I am taking 'A' levels soon and I don't want to jeopardise my chances. The examiners might get to hear about my political affiliations.

The Bad Old Days

BERT BAXTER:

When I was just your age, son, When I was just a
Len-in's my he - ro still, boy, He was a man of

lad, Things were far diffe-rent then I can tell you my friend—They were
steel: If he came back to - day His hair would turn grey At the

ten times   as   bad!   Had me   no gil - ded
whole lou - sy   deal!   Paid up   and joined the

youth,   boy,   Lit by   no sun - shine rays —   We were
par - ty,   Car-ried   the big   red   flag: We were

four-teen in a   hov- el, Tak- in' les - sons how to gro - vel, In the bad   old
com-rades in an ar-my, Though they told us we were bar-my, In the bad   old

days.

days.

DANCE BREAK

27

We toiled our youth a -

28

way, boy — No mon-ey, no thanks, no praise: They say

'Where there's muck there's brass' I say 'Not on your bloom - in' arse!" They were

bad old days.

Your Hair of Gold

GEORGE

Your hair of gold,
   your eyes of baby blue –
How could I ever face
   a life without you?
Your lips so sweet,
   your touch so tender –
You know I surrender to
   everything that you do.

Your glance, your smile –
   they haunt me all the while,
Sleeping or waking you're
   always there beside me.
Your laugh, your kiss –
   my riches forever:
You know that I'll never
   let you go from my heart.

Sunday March 15th
SECOND IN LENT

The house is very quiet. My father sits in the spare room smoking and my mother sits in the bedroom smoking. They are not eating much.

Mr Lucas has phoned my mother three times. All she says to him is, 'Not yet, it's too early.' Perhaps he has asked her to go to the pub for a drink and take her mind off her troubles.

My father has put the stereo in his bedroom. He is playing his Jim Reeves records and staring out of the window. I took him a cup of tea and he said, 'Thanks, son', in a choked-up voice.

My mother was looking at old letters in my father's handwriting when I took her tea in; she said, 'Adrian, what must you think of us?' I said that Rick Lemon, the youth leader, thinks divorce is society's fault. My mother said, 'Bugger society.'

My parents' marriage has always been based on deceit.

My mother's 'hair of gold' comes out of a bottle, but it is only in recent years that she has had the courage to leave the bottle on the bathroom window-sill instead of hiding it at the back of the airing cupboard. My desolated father soon recovered from my mother's extra-marital. He fell tempestuously in love with an unsuitable woman at work and was soon enjoying sexual congress with her. But then my father is a secret romantic. When he's tidying the autumn garden he always picks up the rose petals by hand and puts them into a brass jar in the hall. I have never cross-questioned him about his strange behaviour, but I suspect that it has got something to do with believing that rose petals are fairies' umbrellas. Scoff if you may, but this is my honest opinion.

Another romantic trait of my father's is to listen to American 'Country and Western' singers, mawkishly singing lamentable songs about motorbike crashes and dying dogs, and pure women who run away with cardsharps.

Every Sunday, after he's washed the car, and before he settles down to watch the old Hollywood films on the telly, we have to listen to the same dirge-like ditties on his 'Dansette'. His eyes cloud with tears, he lights a cheroot with trembling hands, his Midlands accent takes on a Western drawl. It is a sickening spectacle.

Thank God I am an intellectual and have discovered Bach.

Your Hair of Gold

Slow

GEORGE: Your hair of gold, of gold, your they
glance, your smile — your

eyes of ba - by blue — How could I ev - er
haunt me all the while: Sleep - ing or wak - ing you're

face a life with - out you? Your lips so sweet, your
al - ways there be - side me: Your laugh, so your kiss — my

touch so ten - der, You know I sur - ren - der to
rich - es for - ev - er: You know that I'll nev - er

Family Trio

Saturday March 14th

It is official. They are getting a divorce! Neither of them wants to leave the house so the spare room is being turned into a bedsitter for my father. This could have a very bad effect on me. It could prevent me from being a vet.

My mother gave me five pounds this morning and told me not to tell my father. I bought some 'Bio-spot' cream for my skin, and the new Abba LP.

I rang Mr Cherry and said I had personal problems and would be unable to work for a few weeks. Mr Cherry said that he knew that my parents were divorcing because my father had cancelled my mother's Cosmopolitan.

My father gave me five pounds, and told me not to tell my mother. I spent it on purple writing paper, and matching envelopes.

Ha! Ha! Ha! . . . to think I once wanted to become a vet! In my maturity I have now gone completely off animals. They are nothing but trouble. I still retain some vestige of affectionate feeling for our dog, but only just.

The period of my parents' estrangement proved to be a formative time for me. It was a waterwheel in my life. How would I develop as a person after going through such agonising traumas? Would I crack under the strain and end up in a home for the teenage maladjusted? Or would I manfully struggle through the dark clouds?

Well, I won't keep you in suspense any longer, gentle reader. As I think is evident from my prose style, I am now a well-balanced person with a gigantic vocabulary. Also I am caring and compassionate towards those lesser mortals with whom I am forced to spend my time. In fact I am a very superior sort of person and I wait impatiently for the rest of the world to recognise the fact.

However, I have developed a very ambivalent attitude towards marriage:

Marriage by A. Mole

Marriage? Huh!
Marriage? Come off it!
Marriage? Oh yeah!
Marriage? Do me a favour!
Marriage? Ha!
Marriage? Pull the other one!
Marriage? Perhaps.
Marriage? Oh yes.
Marriage? Forever.

ADRIAN
Two o'clock in the morning:
Leicester's asleep as sound as a log.
I count sheep in the stillness
As we lie awake – just me and the dog.

PAULINE
Maybe this is the right time to
Find out what I am good for,
And what would be really good for me –
Maybe . . . maybe
I'm more, more than I bargained for,
Braver than I believed I could
Be – I'm free to become . . . who knows?
We'll see, maybe.

GEORGE
Your hair of gold, your eyes of baby blue –
How could I ever face a life without you?

ADRIAN
Five o'clock in the morning:
No-one's about, not even a mouse.
All peace and quiet on the outside –
Who would believe there's a war in our house?

PAULINE
Maybe this is the right time to
Find out what I am good for,
And what would be really good for me –
Maybe . . . maybe
I'm more, more than I bargained for,
Braver than I believed I could
Be – I'm free to become . . . who cares?
We'll see, maybe . . .

GEORGE
Your hair of gold, your eyes of baby blue –
How could I ever face a life without you?
Your lips so sweet, your touch so tender:
You know I surrend to everything that you do.

ADRIAN
Five o'clock in the morning:
No-one's about, not even a mouse.
Nothing moves in the silence –
Who would believe there's a war in our house?

ALL
Maybe . . . maybe . . . maybe . . . maybe . . . we'll see!

Moderato

ADRIAN:

Two o' - clock in the morn - ing: Leices - ter's a-

- sleep as sound as a log. I count sheep in the

still - ness, As we lie a - wake — just me

PAULINE: May - be this is the right time to Find out

ADRIAN: and the dog.

what I am good for, And what would be real - ly good for me— May - be...

may - be— I'm more, more than I bar - gained for, Bra - ver

38

Find out what I am good for, And what would be real-ly good for me

PAULINE: May - be... may - be I'm more, more than I bar - gained for,

GEORGE: Your hair of gold, your

Bra - ver than I be - lieved I could Be, I'm free to be - come...who cares?

eyes of ba - by blue: How could I ev - er

Your Dead Grandad

GRANDMA

I don't recall just when he popped the
    question;
I'm not exactly sure he ever did!
He bought a ring – I've still got that;
We hired the hall, he hired a top hat –
He looked a toff, your dead grandad.

He never had to tell me that he loved me –
We had no use for sentimental chat;
I'd wash the dishes – he would dry,
We dug the garden – time passed by;
I miss him still, your dead grandad.

We never made excuses for bad manners,
No psycho-this or socio-that at all:
Folk were either sane or mad,
We'd no posh words for being bad –
But he was good, your dead grandad.

My grandma told my father off for growing a beard. She said, 'You may think it amusing to look like a communist, George, but I don't.' She said that even in the trenches in Ypres my grandad had shaved every day. Sometimes he had to stop rats from eating his shaving soap. She said that my grandad was even shaved by the undertaker when lying in his coffin, so if the dead could shave there was no excuse for the living.

My father tried to explain, but Grandma didn't stop talking once so it was a bit difficult.

We were both glad when she went home.

My grandma gets older every day, but she has still got a straight back and piercing eyes. She spurns Meals on Wheels and other such aids to the elderly. She doesn't even use her pensioners' bus pass because she walks everywhere.

She was almost mugged last year. The mugger came up behind her and shouted 'Give me your money!' Grandma turned round, looked him full in the eye and said, 'Give me your money, *please*!' This so unnerved the mugger that he ran off, dropping his wallet.

Grandma is always talking about my dead grandad, and his photo is on the sideboard next to a vase of dried flowers. The only clear memory I have of him is of a dwarf-like man wearing a suit and a stiff collar and paisley tie, sitting in an armchair reading *The News Of The World*. He moved his lips as he read about choirboys being deflowered by organists. His voice was thin and squeaky, and he smoked a big pipe. According to Grandma I used to get on his nerves. I was always asking him questions. But he never answered my lisped enquiries.

I once asked Grandma why this was. 'How could he answer your daft questions?' she said, 'He didn't know anything.' On reflection I can see that she was right. If the only newspaper you read is *The News Of The World*, then your grasp of world affairs is bound to be minimal.

I am a dutiful grandson and I visit my grandma as often as I can. I like sitting in her dark house listening to the grandfather clock ticking away in the background. Also my grandma is never too busy to make proper meals, with gravy and custard.

Another thing I like is that you know exactly where you are with Grandma. She has had the same opinions for seventy years: foreigners are dishonest; never trust a person whose eyebrows meet in the middle; the best way to cure a sore throat is to wrap a sweaty sock around the neck; baldness can be prevented by rubbing the scalp with a raw onion, etc . . .

Grandma never says anything, but I sometimes suspect she is lonely for my grandad. Why else would she wash and iron his paisley tie every week? He has been dead for ten years.

Your Dead Grandad

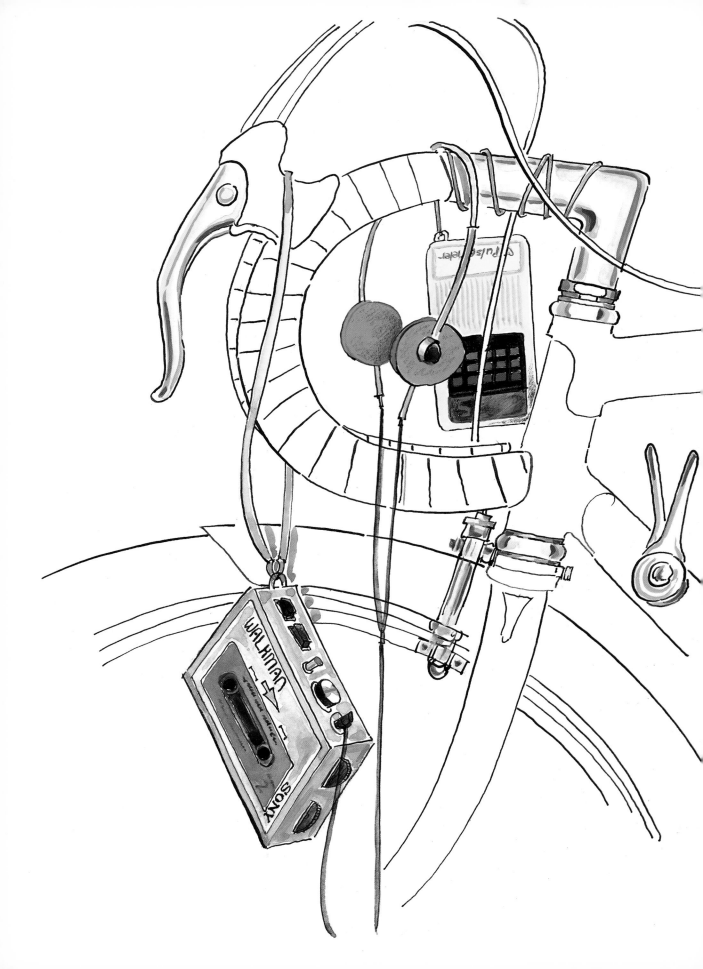

Get It Right!

NIGEL

Adrian Mole, why d'you look such a right arsehole?
I've never seen anyone dress worse!
Your bottoms are flared and your boots curl up
  like they're scared
And your duffel coat positively festers!
Your jumper is straight off the tip –
Do you wear it in bed when you kip?
Oh, Moley, you're wholly, completely – words
  defeat me!
Try Lacoste, Doc Martens, some Farahs you'd
  look smart in –
If you want to wear clothes – get them right!

Your bike's a disgrace, you need a BMX or a racer
With a speedo and ten gears like my one.
This Walkman will surprise you, got a built-in
  graphic equaliser,
With these new lightweight phones – why not try one?
This digital Seiko's for you
If you want to play chess in the loo:
Oh, Mole-face, it's as simple as squeezing a pimple!
Ask for Raleigh, or Sony, Tacchini, Cerutti –
Whatever you get – get it right!

Your taste, I must say, falls far short of
  a true gourmet –
You live on baked beans and fish fingers:
In a hurry a curry from a tin saves a lot of worry,
But it does have a strong pong that lingers.
The best things are subtle, not loud
And known to a few, not the crowd:
Not your Tizer from Tesco – Frascati, al fresco!
Say Martini, say Campari, say Adidas, say Atari,
Say Honda, Sekonda, aerobics, Jane Fonda –
If you want to get on – get it right!

Nigel is dead lucky. His house is absolutely fantastic! Everything is modern. I don't know what he must think of our house; some of our furniture is over a hundred years old!

His bedroom is massive and he has got a stereo, a colour *television, a tapedeck, a Scalextric track, an electric guitar and amplifier, spotlights over his bed, black walls and a white carpet, and a racing car continental quilt. He has got loads of back issues of* Big and Bouncy *so we looked through them. Then Nigel had a cold shower while I cooked the soup and cut the French loaf. We had a good laugh at* Waiting for Godot. *Nigel had hysterics when I said that Vladimir and Estragon sounded like contraception pills.*

I had a go on Nigel's racing bike. I now want one more than anything in the world. If I had to choose between Pandora and a racing bike, I would choose the bike. Sorry, Pandora, but that's how things are.

What a despicable materialist I was then! How I lusted over consumer durables! Of course now, with the onset of age and wisdom, I know that such fripperies only serve to blind us to what the really important things in life are: art, culture and increasing our word power. Nigel is still my best friend, even though he has voluntarily only read one book in his life: *Success and How To Be One* by Simon Bond.

Poor Nigel has had a lot of trouble on deciding which kind of sexuality to opt for: hetero, bi, or homo. He never *could* make up his mind. He is still in the grip of consumerism, and is always changing his stereo system for something more technologically advanced. Personally, myself, I think it is a waste of time. Nigel's bedroom is only twelve feet by sixteen and a half, so what's the point of having a stereo that is powerful enough to be heard in the Urals?

One thing that puzzles me about Nigel: how does he *know* when a fashion is passé? Has he got a spy on the King's Road who telephones news of what's 'in' and what's 'out'? Mind you, I have to concede that Nigel has got charisma; he brings a bottle of Perrier water to sixth form college every day. He drinks three-quarters of it during morning break and saves the rest to wash his face in at lunchtime.

Nigel has never had a teenage spot during the whole of his life, so perhaps Perrier is the answer.

I might give it a go.

Get It Right!

tip —
you

Do you wear it in bed when you kip?
If you want to play chess in the loo:

Oh Mol - ey, you're whol - ly, com - plete - ly — words de - feat me! Try
Oh Mole - face it's as sim - ple as squeez - ing a pim - ple! Ask for

rall.

La - coste, Doc Mar - tens, some Fa - rahs, you'd look smart in — If you want to wear
Ra - leigh, or So - ny, Tac - chi - ni, Ce - rut - ti — What - ev - er you

clothes — get them right! Your
get — get it right! Your

1.2

⊕ CODA

best things are subt-le, — not loud, And known to a few, not the

crowd: Not your Ti - zer from Tes - co — Fras - ca - ti, al fres - co! Say Mar-

- ti - ni, say Cam - pa - ri, say Ad - i - das, say A - ta - ri, Say Hon - da, Se - kon - da, ae -

Gradual accel. e cresc. to end

- ro - bics, Jane Fon - da — if you want to get on — get it right!

Dog

ADRIAN

You are my only true friend,
Always here at the end
Of a traumatic day.
I'm used to your slobbering embrace
And your lop-sided face . . . is OK.

Oh, Dog, never gave you a name,
Still I'm glad that you came
To the house where I live.

You are so easy to please,
And occasional fleas
Don't detract from your charms.
I s'pose you're a bit of a mess,
But I couldn't care less – in my arms

Oh, Dog, you're so floppy and warm!
We'll both weather the storm
In the house where we live.

Sunday January 18th
SECOND AFTER EPIPHANY. OXFORD HILARY TERM STARTS

Mrs Lucas and my mother have had a row over the dog. Somehow it escaped from the house and trampled on Mrs Lucas's wet concrete. My father offered to have the dog put down, but my mother started to cry so he said he wouldn't. All the neighbours were out in the street washing their cars and listening. Sometimes I really hate that dog!

On perusing my 1981 memoirs I note that my entries about the dog are mainly to do with the trouble it caused. This does not give a fair or accurate picture. The dog also caused heartbreak and anguish. But I blame my father for the dog's behavioural difficulties; it received no training during its puppyhood. In my father's own words, 'I just bunged it into a cardboard box, fed it four times a day and took it to the pub when I felt like it.' My mother is not to blame for the dog's neglect; she was completely absorbed in looking after me. By all accounts I was a difficult baby, demanding food and attention at all hours of the day and night (I was especially wakeful during the hours of midnight and 5.00 a.m.).

So the dog and I grew up together. I have never known what it's like to wake up in my own room without having its hairy, slobbering muzzle shoved into my face.

Since I attained the age of reason (in my case ten years of age), I have endeavoured to train the dog to become a responsible canine citizen. But I fear to no avail. The dog is headstrong and impulsive and resists any kind of discipline (a bit like my mother). However it is also kind, tolerant, and warm on cold nights. Another advantage is that the dog doesn't tell me about its boring dreams, unlike other persons who live in this house.

Dog

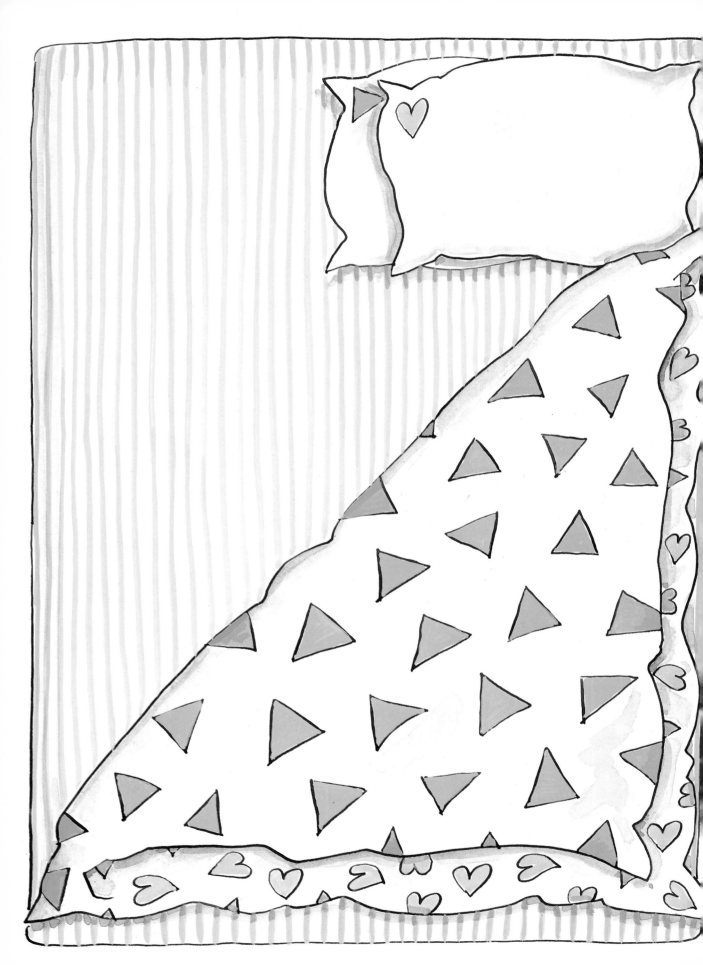

The Other Woman

DOREEN

The other woman – *his* other woman:
I'm another woman in the hours he spends with me.
'The Other Woman' – why does it bother me?
You'd think by now I'd play my old familiar role
  with some good grace.

Now, for a week or two,
I'll pretend he'll stay with me –
Such hurried ecstasy!
Then she'll reappear, he'll say 'Sorry, my dear,
  it was fun' –
And out will go the sun.

The other woman: who *is* 'The Other Woman'?
Who has shown concern for him?
  Deserves his trust and love?
The other woman, *this* other woman,
While she ran out on him, without a thought,
  without a backward glance.

Who came to rescue him,
Soothed away all his pain,
Made him feel brave again?
This other woman, who secretly knew from the start
That he would break my heart.

My father rang Doreen Slater up and she came round straight away. She had a horrible little kid called Maxwell with her. It was quite a shock to see Doreen Slater for the first time. Why my father wanted to have carnal knowledge of her I can't imagine. She is as thin as a stick insect. She has got no bust and no bum. She is just straight all the way up and down, including her nose and mouth and hair. She put her arms round my father as soon as she came into the house. Then she cooked a sloppy sort of meal made with spaghetti and cheese. She is a one-parent family; Maxwell was born out of wedlock. She told me about herself when we were washing up. She would be quite nice if she were a bit fatter.

I know it is unchivalrous of me but I have called Doreen 'Stick Insect' since the first day I saw her. (Not to her thin face, of course.) Poor Stick Insect has had a tragic life worthy of an opera plot. She has suffered from being a man's plaything in the nursery of life. She is like those wobbly toys that won't stay down, but bounce back as soon as you lift a restraining hand. The trouble is that Stick Insect never bounces back to the same man, because they have gone back to their wives, or spurned Doreen's dubious charms for those of a Barbie Doll look-alike.

During one of our long in-depth conversations, I advised Doreen to get an education before her few charms have faded, but Doreen spurned my advice saying, 'I 'ated school, everybody called me "sparrow legs", even the teachers.' I patiently explained that further education teachers were not allowed to mock the physical characteristics of their mature students. But Stick Insect turned peevishly to the beauty tips column of the magazine she was reading and so the subject was closed.

My father was in a long line of Stick Insect's lovers. It's true that he stood by her when she gave birth to Brett Mole, my half-brother, but since then in my opinion he has behaved like a cad. He is always behind with his maintenance money, and never remembers Brett's birthday.

Poor Stick Insect, always the other woman in the triangle of human relationships.

The Other Woman

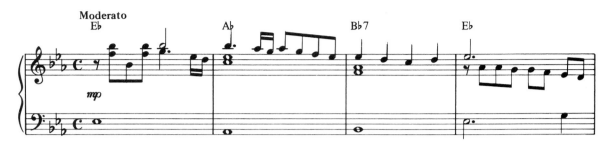

DOREEN SLATER: The oth-er___ wom-an ___ his oth - er
The oth-er ___ wom-an:___ Who is "the oth - er

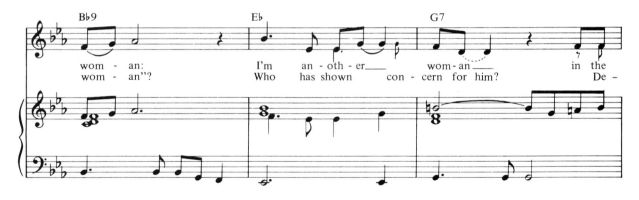

wom - an: I'm an-oth-er___ wom-an ___ in the
wom - an"? Who has shown con-cern for him? De -

hours he spends with me: "The oth - er___
- serves his trust and love? The oth - er___

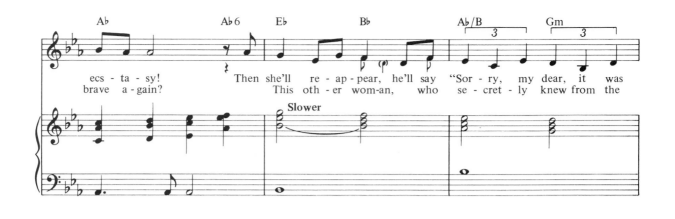

ec - ta - sy! Then she'll re - ap - pear, he'll say "Sor - ry, my dear, it was
brave a - gain? This oth - er wom-an, who se - cret - ly knew from the

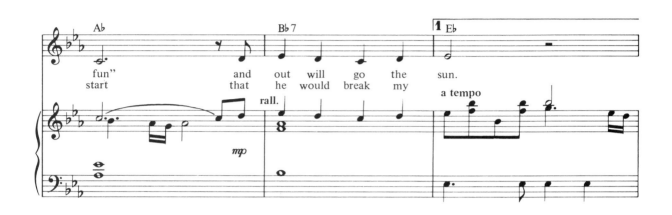

fun" and out will go the sun.
start that he would break my heart.

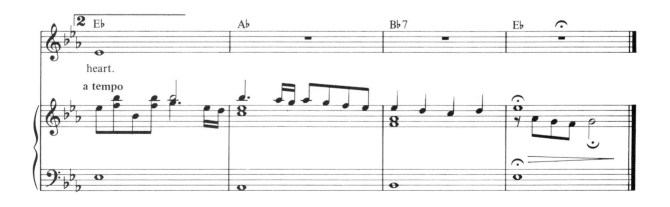

heart.

Oh, Pandora

ADRIAN
Oh, Pandora, I adore . . . ya!
From the first day that I saw ya
I felt destiny called,
I knew I was enthralled
By your aura of love – my Pandora!

Always wondered how it would be;
This is passion as it should be!
Your lips smoulder with fire,
Your eyes melt with desire!
Take me higher and higher, my Pandora!

We'll get married straight away,
Find a cottage by a stream,
With a private wishing-well
Where I can dream
Of my Pandora . . .!

PANDORA
Haven't done my physics homework;
There's that film I want to see on El Salvador –
It must be Channel Four:
There's so much I have to do
If I am to fulfil my potential –
Mustn't waste a second of my time!

Get my 'O's and 'A's – then Oxford!
Take a double first in Law and Economy –
Dead right for an MP!
Spare an afternoon a week
For a lover or two, but no attachment,
Nothing to deflect me from my course!

ADRIAN
Two hearts beat in unison,
Two souls joined in perfect peace,
Our two bodies cry out loud
For release . . .!

Wednesday June 10th

Pandora and I are in love! It is official! She told Claire Neilson, who told Nigel, who told me.
I told Nigel to tell Claire to tell Pandora that I return her love. I am over the moon with joy and rapture. I can overlook the fact that Pandora smokes five Benson and Hedges a day and has her own lighter. When you are in love such things cease to matter.

A smile ripples across my face as I read the above words. How naive I was to think that I could overlook Pandora's loathsome tobacco addiction. She is now, four years later, up to seven cigarettes a day. I have pleaded and cajoled, I have joined ASH, the non-smokers' club, and passed on their mortality statistics and awesome posters, but nothing will persuade Pandora to kick the habit. Her parents are in despair.

I still love Pandora of course, and she still loves me. I admire her brain enormously. Also she is passionately attached to saving seals and other endangered species. Altogether she is an admirable girl who, incidentally, (although it is hardly worth mentioning) has got a voluptuous figure. Our relationship has had its stormy moments, but then we are both temperamental artistes so it is to be expected. I still, secretly, yearn for the marriage bed after the hurly-burly of the recreation ground park bench. But Pandora is going up to Oxford eventually, so our plans are as yet unformed. I doubt if my 'A' level results will be good enough for me to join her in the town of slumbering spires. Indeed I fear that I may lose her to some chinless wimp who is fluent in Latin, Greek and Sanskrit. However, enough of my worries. Pandora and I have enjoyed some good years together. My heart still does a triple somersault whenever I see her assertive figure march into view.
Oh God! . . . Oh Pandora!

GASES AND ATOMS
VOLTA - GUERICKE

Oh, Pandora

ADRIAN: Oh, Pan-

dor - a,   I a - dore... ya: From the
won - dered   how it would   be: This is

first   day_____   that I   saw   ya   I felt
pas - sion_____   as it   should   be!   Your lips

des - ti - ny called   I   knew   I was en-thralled_____   by your
smoul - der with fire,   your eyes   melt   with de-sire!_____   Take me

PANDORA:

Have - n't done my Phy - sics home-work: There's that film I want to see on
'A's' then Ox - ford Take a dou - ble first in law and

ADRIAN:

- do - ra....

El Sal - va - dor It must be Chan-nel Four:
E - co - no - my dead right for an M. P.!

There's so much I have to do if I am to ful - fil my___ pot - en - tial.
Spare an af - ter - noon, a week, for a lov - er or two, but no___ at - tach - ment,

Must - n't waste__ a sec - ond of__ my time!
Noth-ing to__ de -

Get my 'O's' and -flect me from__ my course!

Two hearts beat in un - is - on, two souls

joined in per - fect peace: Our two bod - ies cry out

loud for re - lease!....._____ Oh please Pan -

PANDORA: Have-n't done my phy-sics home-work: There's that film I want to see on -do-ra I im-plore ya.

ADRIAN: -do-ra I im-plore ya. From the

El Sal-va-dor It must be Chan-nel Four:

first___ day that I saw ya I felt

There's so much I have to do if I am to ful-fil my___ pot-en-tial

des-ti-ny called, I knew I was en-thralled_____ by your

The Young Girl Inside You

Saturday January 16th
MOON'S LAST QUARTER

Bert got married today.

The Alderman Cooper Sunshine Home hired a coach and took the old ladies to form a guard of honour with their walking frames.

Bert looked dead good. He cashed his life insurance in and spent the money on a new suit. Queenie was wearing a hat made of flowers and fruit. She had a lot of orange make-up on her face to try and cover the wrinkles.

Queenie Baxter was a thrice-married widow when she was admitted to the Alderman Cooper Sunshine Home. She had no physical impediments but her social worker thought she was too absent-minded to be able to live alone. Queenie swept Bert off his feet (not difficult considering that by now Bert was in a wheelchair). Queenie set out to seduce Bert. She took him for long walks around the Leisure Centre; she tempted him with de-crusted beetroot sandwiches; she lavished attention on Sabre, Bert's awesome Alsatian. She fed him Dog-o-chocks (Sabre, not Bert). Soon Bert's head was in a whirlpool, his old crusty hormones were stirred and he fell head first into lust, then love, then marriage.

At the time it was all very puzzling to me; I had always thought that people over thirty stopped falling in love. So it was a revolution to me to find passion amongst my geriatric acquaintances.

Grandma always gets a funny look in her eye whenever she clasps her eyes on Ned Herrin, the fishmonger. In the past I have put it down to the smell of the fish, but perhaps there is something stirring between old Ned, Grandma and the fish heads.

Bert and Queenie enjoyed a happy marriage in their pensioners' bungalow. Bert even learned to accept the 697 glass animals that Queenie insisted on scattering about their tiny living-room. At certain times of the day if the light was right and she was laughing, Queenie looked like a very young girl.

QUEENIE
When you look in the mirror
The person reflected
Is a stranger you don't know
And don't care to meet.
But the young girl inside you
Is bright-eyed and flirty,
Not a day over thirty,
Who longs to be loved.

Why does youth think it odd
That those older than God
Should know the pangs of desire,
Feel the flames of love's fire?
It's not strange, it's not odd
'Cause inside these old bodies
Our younger selves live
Just as lusty as you.

(*Wheelchair gavotte*)

QUEENIE AND BERT
Why does youth think it odd
That those older than God
Should know the pangs of desire,
Feel the flame of love's fire?
It's not strange, it's not odd
'Cause inside these old bodies
Our younger selves live
Just as lusty as you.

With a lilt

QUEENIE: When you look in the mir - ror the per - son re - flect - ed is a stran - ger you don't know and don't care to meet: But the young girl in - side you is bright - eyed and flir - ty, Not a day ov - er thir - ty, who longs to be loved. Why does

69

youth think it odd that those old - er than God should know pangs of de -

- sire,____ feel the flame of love's fire? It's not strange, it's not odd 'cause in-

-side these old bo - dies our young - er selves live just as lus - ty as

you.

Wheelchair Gavotte

Coming Down to Earth Again

PAULINE

Coming down to earth again,
Out of sunshine into twilight;
Coming down to earth again
From my rocket flight.

Coming down to earth again,
Terra firma out of the sky;
Coming round on earth again –
Touch-down from on high.

I've had my fling; I let my hair right down –
I dreamed that I could survive without ties:
Dreaming was fine, but now it's wake-up time
And I'm rubbing the sleep from my eyes.

Hello the life I thought I'd shed for good
And hello people I'd blocked from my mind:
After the wine at last it's own-up time
In the world I left behind.

Coming down to earth again,
I'm back home – coming in – coming home . . .

Sunday November 29th
ADVENT SUNDAY

My mother has just turned up with no warning! She had all her suitcases with her. She has thrown herself on the mercy of my father. My father has thrown himself on the body of my mother. I tactfully withdrew to my bedroom where I am now trying to work out how I feel about my mother's return. On the whole I am over the moon, but I'm dreading her looking around our squalid house. She will go mad when she finds out that I have lent Pandora her fox-fur coat.

'On the whole I am over the moon': that was a chronic understatement. I was beside myself with gibbering joy. Naturally at that age my emotions were repressed. I have since learnt that there is nothing wrong with displaying your emotions in public. So I now occasionally touch my mother's arm in passing. It seems to please her and it costs me nothing. I expect it was difficult for her to leave her wild life in Sheffield where she was a mistress in a flat and return to be a wife and a mother in a cul-de-sac. But I'm glad she made the decision to return to us.

My mother is not like the mothers on television; she doesn't care how white she can wash P.E. shorts, and she hardly ever remembers to rinse the milk bottles out. Still there is more to life than P.E. shorts and milk bottles and my mother has got some good points: she laughs a lot, she is a good speller, and she is kind to animals. That's about it, really.

Sometimes my mother stops halfway through laughing and looks sad; it could be that she has noticed that the house needs redecorating, or it could be latent regrets that cause her mood change.

When I am rich and famous I will pay somebody to decorate our house; I will also fork out for a face-lift for her.

That should keep her smiling.

Coming Down to Earth Again

Com-ing round on earth a - gain Touch-down from on high.

I've had my fling:_ I let my hair right down, I dreamed that I could sur - vive_ with-out
Hel - lo the life_ I thought I'd shed for good and hel - lo peo - ple I'd blocked from my

ties:_
mind:_

Dream-ing was fine_ but now it's wake-up time_ and I'm
Af - ter the wine_ at last it's own-up time_ in the

rub - bing the sleep from my eyes.

75

The Adrian Mole Theme